anythink

D0601762

FRONT LOADERS SCOOP!

by Beth Bence Reinke

BUMBA BOOKS™

LERNER PUBLICATIONS ◆ MINNEAPOLIS

Note to Educators:

Throughout this book, you'll find critical thinking questions. These can be used to engage young readers in thinking critically about the topic and in using the text and photos to do so.

Lerner Publications Company
A division of Lerner Publishing Group, Inc.
241 First Avenue North
Minneapolis, MN 55401 USA

For reading levels and more information, look up this title at www.lernerbooks.com.

Library of Congress Cataloging-in-Publication Data

Names: Reinke, Beth Bence, author.
Title: Front loaders scoop! / by Beth Bence Reinke.
Description: Minneapolis : Lerner Publications, [2018] | Series: Bumba books. Construction zone | Audience: Age 4–7. | Audience: K to Grade 3. | Includes bibliographical references and index.
Identifiers: LCCN 2016044750 (print) | LCCN 2016050325(ebook) | ISBN 9781512433609 (lb : alk. paper) | ISBN 9781512455441 (pb : alk. paper) | ISBN 9781512450248 (eb pdf)
Subjects: LCSH: Loaders (Machines)—Juvenile literature.
Classification: LCC TL296.5 .R44 2018 (print) | LCC TL296.5 (ebook) | DDC 621.8/6—dc23

LC record available at https://lccn.loc.gov/2016044750

Manufactured in the United States of America
1—CG—7/15/17

LERNER
SOURCE

Expand learning beyond the printed book. Download free, complementary educational resources for this book from our website, www.lernerresource.com.

Table of
Contents

Front Loaders

Front loaders work at

construction sites.

Their wide buckets scoop

heavy loads.

treads

Front loaders drive over the bumpy ground.

Their tires have treads.

Treads help the loader grip the ground.

Why might front loaders need to grip the ground?

The driver sits in the cab.

He controls the loader's arms.

The bucket is at the end of the arms.

teeth

The bucket has teeth.

Teeth cut into the earth.

The bucket scoops up dirt.

The arms lift the bucket.

How do you think the loader's teeth cut into the earth?

The arms tip the bucket.

The dirt spills into a

dump truck.

The dump truck will haul

the dirt away.

Front loaders can scoop

rocks and sand too.

Some loaders move trash.

Front loaders can be huge.

Sometimes the driver has to

climb a ladder to the cab.

Some front loaders are small.

The smallest kind is called a

skid loader.

Skid loaders work in small spaces.

What kinds of jobs could skid loaders do?

Front loaders scoop and dump

big loads.

They work hard to get the job done.

Parts of a Front Loader

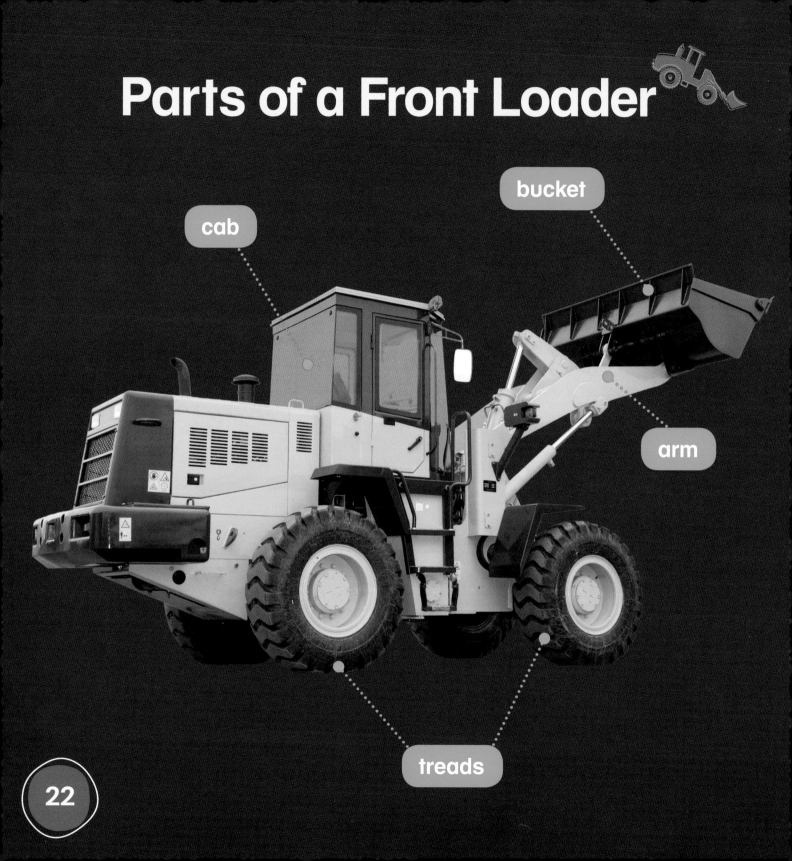

cab

bucket

arm

treads

Picture Glossary

construction sites

places where construction, or building, takes place

skid loader

a small kind of front loader used for smaller jobs

teeth

sharp metal points on the edge of the bucket

treads

ridges on tires that help them grip the earth and keep them from slipping

23

Read More

Hill, Lee Sullivan. *Earthmovers on the Move*. Minneapolis: Lerner Publications, 2011.

Lennie, Charles. *Loaders*. Minneapolis: ABDO Kids, 2015.

Reinke, Beth Bence. *Bulldozers Push!* Minneapolis: Lerner Publications, 2018.

Index

Photo Credits